WHAT MAKES A RAPHAEL A RAPHAEL?

Richard Mühlberger

The Metropolitan Museum of Art
Viking
NEW YORK

VIKING
First published in 1993 by The Metropolitan Museum of Art, New York, and Viking, a division of Penguin Books USA Inc., 375 Hudson Street, New York, New York 10014, U.S.A. and Penguin Books Canada Ltd., 2801 John Street, Markham, Ontario, Canada L3R 1B4

Produced by the Department of Special Publications,
The Metropolitan Museum of Art
Series Editor: Mary Beth Brewer
Front Cover Design: Marleen Adlerblum
Design: Nai Y. Chang
Printing and Binding: A. Mondadori, Verona, Italy

Library of Congress Cataloging-in-Publication Data
Mühlberger, Richard. What makes a Raphael a Raphael? / Richard Mühlberger.
p. cm.
"The Metropolitan Museum of Art."
Summary: Explores such art topics as style, composition, color, and subject matter as they relate to twelve works by Raphael.
ISBN 0-87099-671-1 (MMA) ISBN 0-670-85204-X (Viking)
1. Raphael, 1483–1520—Criticism and interpretation—Juvenile literature. 2. Painting, Italian—Juvenile literature. 3. Painting, Renaissance—Italy—Juvenile literature. [1. Raphael, 1483–1520. 2. Painting, Italian. 3. Art appreciation.] I. Metropolitan Museum of Art (New York, N.Y.) II. Title.
ND623.R2M85 1993 759.5—dc20 93-7579 CIP AC
10 9 8 7 6 5 4 3 2

ILLUSTRATIONS

Unless otherwise noted, all works are by Raphael.

Pages 1 and 2: *The Madonna and Child with the Infant Baptist*, oil on panel, 15¼ x 12⅞ in., reproduced by courtesy of the Trustees, The National Gallery, London.

Page 6: Detail from *The School of Athens*, fresco, Vatican Palace, Rome; photograph, Vatican Museums.

Page 8: Study from the Palace of Federigo da Montefeltro at Gubbio, Italian, ca. 1476–80, intarsia of walnut, beech, rosewood, oak, and fruitwoods on a walnut base, The Metropolitan Museum of Art, Rogers Fund, 1939, 39.153.

Page 9: Fra Carnevale (Bartolomeo di Giovanni Corradini), Italian (Marchigian), active by 1451, died 1484, *The Birth of the Virgin*, tempera and oil on wood, 57 x 37⅞ in., The Metropolitan Museum of Art, Rogers and Gwynne Andrews Funds, 1935, 35.121.

Page 10: *An Allegory (Vision of a Knight)*, oil on panel, 6¾ x 6¾ in., reproduced by courtesy of the Trustees, The National Gallery, London.

Page 12: Pietro Perugino, *The Marriage of the Virgin*, oil on panel, 92⅛ x 72⅞ in., Musée des Beaux-Arts, Caen; photograph, Giraudon/Art Resource, New York.

Page 13: *The Marriage of the Virgin*, oil on panel, 66⅞ x 46½ in., 1504, Pinacoteca di Brera, Milan; photograph, Nimatallah/Art Resource, New York.

Page 17: *Saint George and the Dragon*, oil on wood, 11⅛ x 8⅜ in., Andrew W. Mellon Collection, © 1993 National Gallery of Art, Washington.

Page 18: *Madonna and Child Enthroned, with Saints*, tempera and gold on wood, main panel, overall, 67⅞ x 67⅞ in., lunette, overall, 29½ x 70⅞ in., The Metropolitan Museum of Art, Gift of J. Pierpont Morgan, 1916, 16.30ab; photograph, Geoffrey Clements.

Page 21: *The Alba Madonna*, oil on wood, transferred to canvas, 37¼ in. diameter, Andrew W. Mellon Collection, © 1993 National Gallery of Art, Washington.

Page 22: *The Madonna and Child with the Infant Baptist*, oil on panel, 15¼ x 12⅞ in., reproduced by courtesy of the Trustees, The National Gallery, London.

Page 22: *The Madonna della Sedia*, oil on panel, 28 in. diameter, Pitti Palace, Florence; photograph, Scala/Art Resource, New York.

Page 23: *The Small Cowper Madonna*, oil on wood, 23⅜ x 17⅜ in., Widener Collection, © 1993 National Gallery of Art, Washington.

Page 23: *Madonna and Child with the Infant St. John*, red chalk, 8 13/16 x 6¼ in., The Metropolitan Museum of Art, Rogers Fund, 64.47.

Page 25: *Galatea*, fresco, 116¼ x 88⅝ in., Palazzo della Farnesina, Rome; photograph, Scala/Art Resource, New York.

Page 29: *The Deliverance of Saint Peter from Prison*, fresco, Vatican Palace, Rome; photograph, Vatican Museums.

Page 32: *Saint Cecilia with Saints Paul, John the Evangelist, Augustine, and Mary Magdalen*, oil on canvas, transferred from panel, 93¾ x 59 in., Pinacoteca di Bologna; photograph, Antonio Guerra, Bologna.

Page 34: *The Miraculous Draught of Fishes*, gouache on paper, 125½ x 157 in., Victoria and Albert Museum, London; photograph, Victoria and Albert Museum/Art Resource, New York.

Page 35: Workshop of Pieter van Aelst (after Raphael), *The Miraculous Draught of Fishes*, tapestry, 193¾ x 201½ in., Vatican Museums, Rome; photograph, Scala/Art Resource, New York.

Page 39: *Portrait of Baldassare Castiglione*, oil on canvas, 32¼ x 26 in., Musée du Louvre, © PHOTO R.M.N.

Page 41: *The Vision of Ezekiel*, oil on panel, 15¾ x 11¾ in., Pitti Palace, Florence; photograph, Scala/Art Resource, New York.

Page 43: *The Transfiguration*, oil on panel, 159½ x 109½ in., Vatican Museum, Rome; photograph, Vatican Museums.

Page 49: *The School of Athens*, fresco, Vatican Palace, Rome; photograph, Vatican Museums.

CONTENTS

Raphael's most celebrated works are a series of murals in the Vatican. In this detail from The School of Athens, *he portrayed himself. He is the young man on the right wearing a black hat and looking out.*

Meet Raffaello Sanzio

Raffaello Sanzio, known to us as Raphael, was born on April 6, 1483, in the Italian town of Urbino. Although a small place, Urbino had become a center of culture under Duke Federigo da Montefeltro, its greatest leader. The duke brought the best artists to Urbino to decorate his palace, where he created a large and wonderful library. One of those artists was Raphael's father, Giovanni Santi, who, in twenty-three books of verse, recorded the deeds of the duke and his ancestors. Federigo da Montefeltro's death occurred just seven months before the birth of Raphael.

Young Raphael's first lessons in art were in the duke's palace, where the walls were covered with scenes in paint and inlaid wood. They showed people, buildings, and landscapes in a new way. Everything seemed real. When he looked at the pictures, Raphael thought he was viewing the world through a window. He could see far, far away, just as he could from the top of the palace tower or from the summit of one of the hills nearby. He was not very old before he learned that the sky, mountains, and trees were only wood or paint on flat areas of wall, as were the quietly dignified people who inhabited the pictures.

What made these pictures so special to young Raphael was that the artists who composed them used the innovative technique of linear perspective to create natural-looking settings filled with people who also looked real. One of the most important rules of the technique is that objects appear to be smaller when they become more distant. First used in Florence, an important city west of Urbino, the use of linear perspective spread fast to other Italian towns during the period known as the Renaissance.

The word Renaissance, which means rebirth, refers to the revival of interest in ancient Greek and Roman learning that began in Italy in the fifteenth century. Many people consider Raphael's paintings the highest expression of Renaissance ideals, and believe that the period came to an end with the artist's untimely death in 1520.

When Raphael was still a boy, he learned to draw and to master perspective. He probably also learned good manners in the court of Urbino, for it was known as one of the most cultivated places in all of Europe. Giovanni Santi realized that his

STUDY FROM THE PALACE OF FEDERIGO DA MONTEFELTRO

Raphael grew up in the palace of the duke of Urbino, who loved learning and the arts. In the duke's private study, the walls were decorated with pictures made out of tiny pieces of wood. Although this detail, from the duke's study in the nearby town of Gubbio, looks like an open cabinet with books and other objects on the shelves, the wall is actually flat. The table under the cabinets, and even the shadows cast by the table legs, are parts of the picture made of wood.

son had exceptional talents. He decided, therefore, to ask Pietro Perugino, a very successful artist in nearby Perugia, to take Raphael as an apprentice. In Perugino's busy studio, the boy would learn everything he needed to know to start a successful career of his own. Not long after these arrangements were made, Raphael's father died. The young artist was eleven years old.

Little is known of Raphael during the next six years, but it is thought that he accompanied Perugino to Florence to learn the Renaissance style at its source. By 1500, Raphael was back in Perugia painting pictures for churches. While he was first starting out as an independent artist—at only seventeen years of age—Raphael remained faithful to his teacher's way of painting. But before long, Raphael's talents grew and matured to such a degree that they were known throughout Italy, and he was called upon to serve the most powerful people of his day.

In Florence, Raphael could see the great works of his idols and rivals, Leonardo da Vinci and Michelangelo, two of the most famous artists of all time. Although Raphael was younger and lived a much shorter life than either Leonardo or Michelangelo, his achievements rank with theirs. All of the great paintings, engravings, mosaics, tapestries, and buildings he designed were created in fewer than twenty years. This book will explore twelve of Raphael's great works that span his career from the start to the last days.

Fra Carnevale
THE BIRTH OF THE VIRGIN

Renaissance artists wanted their paintings to tell stories set in architectural settings that seemed realistic. During his youth in Urbino, Raphael may have seen pictures like this, which shows stately figures and an elegant classical building.

An Allegory (Vision of a Knight)

It is not known who hired Raphael to paint this small panel, known as *An Allegory* or *Vision of a Knight*. Filled with symbols, it is about the education of a young Renaissance knight. In his sleep, he sees a tall bay tree standing between the two paths in life. The soberly dressed figure on the left is Virtue, who holds out a sword and a book to the young man. These objects represent the knight's hope for a successful life as a soldier and scholar. In the background is the house of Virtue, reached only by following winding paths and climbing over high rocks. It is hard to get there, just as the dream she proffers is difficult to obtain. On the right, holding flowers as beautiful as her face and her flowing dress, is Pleasure, who promises the knight something easier. She will lead the youth to love.

The charm that Raphael gave this small painting is its outward simplicity, but a little probing reveals complex layers of meaning. The sleeping knight is Scipio Africanus, a famous soldier from ancient times in Italy. The women are the classical goddesses of wisdom and love, or virtue and pleasure. Renaissance Italians were keenly aware of their glorious Roman ancestors. They studied the books and art of ancient Rome and modeled buildings after those of their forefathers. As a new age was being shaped during the Renaissance, the lessons from previous days had more meaning than ever before.

Balance in Life

Raphael's painting is perfectly symmetrical. The bay tree divides it right down the middle. From the edges of the picture, the women reach over the knight, who is stretched between them. Like objects of equal weight being measured on an old-fashioned scale, everything is in balance. In fact, the word *symmetry* comes from two Greek words that together mean "of like measure." In Renaissance times, a measured, or balanced, life was the goal of every educated person, for it was believed that such a life brought harmony to one's soul.

Raphael emphasized the differences between the goddesses by showing them against contrasting landscapes. On the left is a rocky mound, while on the right are gentle hills that extend farther and farther into the distance. Renaissance artists noticed that the farther away things were, the lighter in color and the fuzzier in outline they appeared. This is because mist, fog, and other kinds of atmospheric conditions between the viewer and objects in the distance make those objects look softer and less detailed. To reproduce this effect in painting, Raphael made the mountains the color of the sky, and made each hill a little fainter than the one in front of it. This technique, called aerial perspective, is yet another way that artists can indicate distance.

The Marriage of the Virgin

Pietro Perugino
THE MARRIAGE OF THE VIRGIN

Raphael was still a teenager when his teacher, Perugino, began this altarpiece for the Cathedral of Perugia. In his painting, Perugino captured the quiet beauty of Mary's marriage to Joseph.

Raphael must have been proud to watch his master Perugino create a painting of the marriage of the Virgin for the Cathedral of Perugia. This elegant and beautiful work, displayed in the most important church in the region, was praised by many. Before long, Raphael was commissioned by a prominent family to paint the same subject for a chapel in a church at Città di Castello, a small town about thirty miles from Perugia. The young artist could think of no better scheme for his painting than the one his teacher had used. He adopted every part of Perugino's composition, from a rounded top to emphasize the nobility of the temple, to the temple's see-through doorway. But in showing such respect and homage to his master, he also outdid him. Raphael's version of the painting was quickly compared to Perugino's and was judged better. It was the young man's first masterpiece.

Using Perspective to Convey Feeling
Raphael used perspective to unify the foreground and the background of his painting. The figures in the foreground are the same height as the temple behind them, but everyone knows that in reality, the people are smaller than the building. Measured in relation to the figures in the background near it, though, the temple is more than ten times human height. Raphael was able to fill

half the painting with figures, and to fit a huge building into the other half by using linear perspective. The people and squares in the pavement become smaller as they recede toward the temple.

Raphael used perspective not only to make his painting look realistic, but also to create a special feeling. He wanted to confer the magnificence of the domed building to the marriage partners. To do so, he used the pavement to link the holy couple to the temple. Starting under their feet, the rectangular shapes march back, ending inside the temple under the dome, a symbol of heaven.

Raphael also sought to express holiness by attempting to paint perfect forms in a perfect setting. He started by applying symmetry to his composition. The temple is centered at the top of the painting and the figures in front are evenly arranged on both sides. Every figure is elegant and beautifully posed. The central figure nods toward Joseph, the only relaxation of Raphael's strict balance.

The Bible does not mention the marriage of Mary and Saint Joseph, but there was a fictional account of the courtship and wedding in a book called *The Golden Legend*. It told that Mary had many suitors, who were asked to line up in the temple to draw rods for her. Among those who stood in line was Joseph, who took a rod just as the others did. Joseph's rod blossomed, God's sign that he was to wed Mary. In Raphael's painting,

When Raphael painted the same subject, he did not copy Perugino exactly. He made his figures taller and the temple more complicated and distant.

Joseph rests the rod on his shoulder, and the other suitors do the same. Only the lad in red tights realizes that his rod is no longer of any use. Joseph, barefooted as a sign of humility, places a wedding ring on Mary's finger.

Raphael's temple in *The Marriage of the Virgin* shows that he was proud of his accomplishments, for across its front he wrote his own name as though it were carved in the marble: RAPHAEL VRBINAS, "Raphael of Urbino."

Details from THE MARRIAGE OF THE VIRGIN
BY **Raphael** (LEFT) AND **Perugino** (RIGHT)

*Faces painted by Raphael and Perugino are very similar. Of course,
people did not all look alike during the Renaissance, but many artists
believed that outer beauty reflected the goodness of one's soul. That is
why they depicted holy people like these with beautiful, ideal faces.*

Saint George and the Dragon

King Henry VII of England made Duke Federigo da Montefeltro a knight in the exclusive Order of the Garter. After the duke's death, the king continued England's close alliance with Urbino by making the duke's son a knight in the order as well. The new duke immediately asked Raphael to paint a picture to give to the king as a token of gratitude. The subject was Saint George, the patron saint of England and of the order.

Raphael chose to paint Saint George's most famous deed, the slaying of a dragon that was terrorizing the countryside and feeding on its inhabitants. Saint George came upon the dragon just as the beast was about to take a young princess as prey. Raphael set the scene outside the dragon's lair, a dark cave. As the monster's eyes lock on those of its adversary and the saint's pure white steed rears up, George thrusts his lance into the dragon's belly. In contrast to this action, the landscape is peaceful. Behind the princess, the rocks above the dragon's cave are balanced by tall, straight trees.

Raphael emphasized the poise and skill of this Christian knight, who believes that God will protect him as he charges the muscular dragon. The flurry of Saint George's blue cape and his fearless concentration as he aims the lance summarize his heroic act. The horse, coming to a rearing halt, twists its head back, a sign that the animal has been trained to obey its master.

Renaissance noblemen, like the duke of Urbino and the king of England, considered the taming of a horse to rear and halt at will to be part of a prince's training. Saint George, therefore, stands for the perfect ruler, and this equestrian picture of him was a fitting gift from the duke to the king. But the story of Saint George represented more than knighthood, gallantry, and the Renaissance prince. After the dragon was killed, the citizens of the town converted to Christianity in thanks for the saint's heroic deed. Saint George stood for the triumph of Christianity over the dark forces of evil.

Unlike many artists before him, Raphael chose not to picture the horse in profile, parallel to the bottom edge of the painting. Instead he used a Renaissance discovery, foreshortening, the contraction of an object to give the illusion that it recedes or projects into space. This device allowed artists to show horses charging toward or away from the viewer. The hindquarters of Saint George's horse are closer to the viewer than the animal's front legs. To make this pose look right, Raphael had to know precisely how much to shorten the horse's body as it turned away from the front of the picture. Foreshortening and perspective go hand in hand. Foreshortening allowed Raphael to place the horse and rider convincingly in the landscape; perspective made his landscape appear to go back into the distance.

Madonna and Child Enthroned, with Saints

The "Royal" Family

A group of nuns in Perugia asked Raphael to paint an altarpiece for the chapel of their convent. On a tall wood panel that was to be placed above an altar, Raphael painted a splendid throne fit for a queen. He placed Mary on it, with Jesus on her lap and Saint John the Baptist, Jesus's cousin, at her knee. The throne elevates the members of this "royal" family so that people far back in the chapel could see them. For the throne's steps, Raphael imitated stark black and white marble with gold inlay. In addition to their rich materials, the steps are designed with an illusionistic trick. Even though we look up at the painting, it seems as if we are looking down at the steps. When worshipers in the chapel went to the altar to pray or receive the Holy Sacrament, they saw the top of each step, a silent invitation to climb stairs that would bring their hearts closer to Mary and her holy son.

Conversing with Saints

Mary tenderly coaxes Saint John to her lap, while Jesus bestows a blessing on him. The figures who stand closest to Mary and Jesus are, on the left, Saint Catherine and, on the right, a saint who may be Cecilia. She carries a palm branch, the sign of a martyr, someone who died for her faith. Saint Catherine also carries a palm branch, announcing her victory over death as a martyr. Catherine's second attribute is distinctive. It is the spiked wheel on which she supports her right hand. This instrument was once used to torture her, but miraculously, it delivered her from injury.

Saint Peter, wearing a yellow robe, dangles an easily recognized symbol from his left hand, the keys to the kingdom of heaven, which Jesus gave to him. Saint Paul, dressed in bright red, is the great writer of the New Testament Epistles. In his right hand he holds his symbol, the sword with which he once persecuted Christians and with which he himself was later martyred after his conversion to Christianity. Above, in the half round panel, or lunette, God the Father looks down and blesses the scene. One of the angels in the lunette looks out at the congregation, as do Saint Peter and the nameless martyr. Their eyes meet the eyes of those who worship, silently urging them to come to the altar.

The Alba Madonna

In ancient times, Rome was the capital of most of Europe and of all the countries bordering the Mediterranean Sea. Many of the magnificent buildings from those days had been destroyed and their ruins built upon by the time Raphael moved there in 1508. But he saw everything of the past that could be found and had a deep respect for it.

A Roman Madonna

In this painting, Raphael copied nothing directly from Roman art, but the nobility of the figures was the result of his study of ancient sculpture. The soft gold and green earth and gentle hills he painted were those of the Roman countryside.

The Madonna frequently is shown sitting on a throne, but when Raphael placed her in the middle of a meadow, she became no less queenly. Because thrones were found mainly in churches and palaces, and because ordinary people sat on stools or on the floor, when Mary was shown sitting on the ground, she was known as the Madonna of Humility. Here, Jesus rests against his mother's lap and holds a cross. Saint John is dressed in a camel's-hair garment like the one he will wear as an adult when he preaches in the wilderness and baptizes people to prepare them for the coming of Jesus. Mary pauses in her reading, for she is sorrowful. The cross reminds her of the suffering that is in store for her son.

A Triangle in a Circle

Raphael held the three silent figures together by arranging them in a triangle. The highest point of this imaginary shape is above Mary's head. One of the triangle's sides is formed partly by her left arm, while her right arm and Saint John's back form the second side and the edge of her robes and her foot form the bottom. Grouping figures in the shape of a triangle was common during the Renaissance. It gave a painting a stable base and a symmetrical composition. Putting the picture into a circle, however, made it unsteady. Round compositions like to roll unless they are in perfect balance. Mary and Jesus lean their heads to the left, so the circle wants to go in that direction. John, facing the opposite way, slows it down, but it is Mary's foot that stops the motion. In this way, she "puts on the brakes." Raphael knew that the thrust of her leg and foot would bring just the right measure of balance to his triangle within a circle.

Raphael's paintings of the Madonna and Child, which sometimes include young Saint

John, are the most beloved of all the artist's works. More than forty of them exist today, and each one is miraculously different from the next. The differences are not simply in faces, costumes, or settings. Raphael made each one unique in the way he balanced the figures and composition. By the nod of a head, the thrust of an arm, the leaning of a child forward or back, and by other subtle but natural movements, he brought infinite variety to Christianity's favorite subject.

THE MADONNA DELLA SEDIA

Here, Raphael harmonized the three figures with the circular shape of the painting by rounding the top of Mary's turban and stressing the curves of her arm, shoulder, and knee. Even Jesus's chubby body echoes the painting's rounded shape.

THE MADONNA AND CHILD WITH THE INFANT BAPTIST

Raphael composed the three family members within a triangle, placing Mary's head at the top. As Mary embraces and protects the two boys, she and Jesus gaze sweetly at Saint John, who offers his cousin a flower.

22

THE SMALL COWPER MADONNA

This vertical composition shows Mary holding Jesus standing up on Mary's lap. Nestled within the lovely, gentle hills in the background is a Renaissance church.

MADONNA AND CHILD WITH THE INFANT SAINT JOHN

Raphael again composed Mary, Jesus, and Saint John in a triangle, with Mary's head at its highest point. Saint John kneels before Jesus, who stands supported by his mother. As Mary leans forward, her skirt billows out, forming the base of the triangle.

Galatea

When Raphael arrived in Rome at the start of the sixteenth century, the city was one of the most important in the world. The Roman Catholic church had been founded there, and the popes who headed it enriched the city, particularly during the Renaissance. Julius II and Leo X, the popes of Raphael's time, liked the young artist's work, and so did many other powerful Romans. Raphael frequently was called upon to add to the city's splendor. One of his patrons was Agostino Chigi, a banker whose stupendous wealth financed kings, states, and the Catholic church. He had just built a villa outside the walls of Rome on the river Tiber, within view of St. Peter's. Chigi asked Raphael to fresco the wall of an arcade over-looking the river. "Fresco" means to paint on plaster while it is wet.

Writers during the Renaissance often found stories in ancient Greek and Roman literature that they liked to tell anew. One of them, the romance of the goddess Galatea, was very popular in Raphael's day, perhaps because Galatea lived off the coast of Italy. In the story, Polyphemus, a fierce, one-eyed giant, falls madly in love with Galatea and pursues her everywhere she goes.

In Raphael's painting, Galatea may escape him, for the boy at the bottom, Palaemon, has guided many sailors out of storms, and the placid sea presents him with easy work. The difficulty is that Cupid's army is out in force. Their arrows awaken love, and they are pointed right at Galatea.

Raphael pictured Galatea standing in a seashell pulled by dolphins. One of her escorts munches an octopus for energy. Galatea and all of her companions are sons and daughters of sea gods. The females are called nereids and the males are known as tritons.

Raphael did not use one particular model for Galatea. He said he based Galatea on "an ideal." Ideal

beauty was something the ancient Greeks sought in their art, and they found it by looking at many beautiful people and making the ideal, or perfect, person out of parts from each of them.

Raphael designed his painting so that Galatea is always the center of attention. No matter where viewers look or how carefully they study a detail, they always return to her. Raphael guaranteed this in a number of ways. Galatea is the only figure in red, a color that demands attention. The cloak streaming out behind the goddess isolates her from the others. She is also in the center of the painting and, by the twist of her body, links the sea with the sky. The triton immediately to her left and the nereid to her right raise their arms toward Galatea's face, detracting from themselves and leading to her. Seven narrow lines formed by the arrows from above and by the reins that link her hands to the dolphins are also aimed at Galatea. Centered above her head, the design made by the flying cupids and their bows acts like a canopy, directing attention to Galatea.

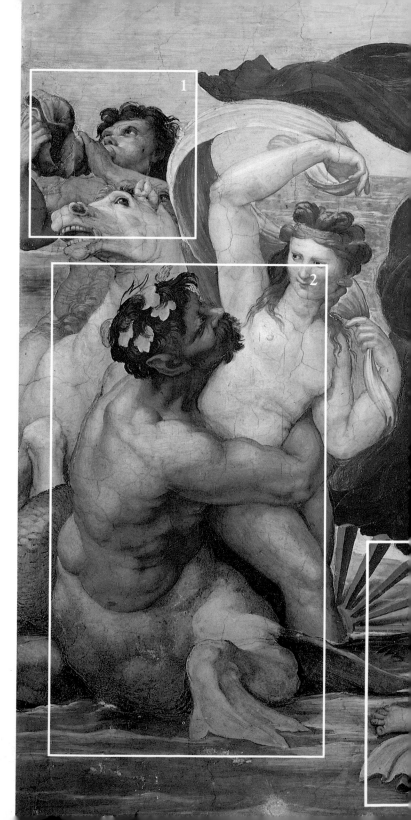

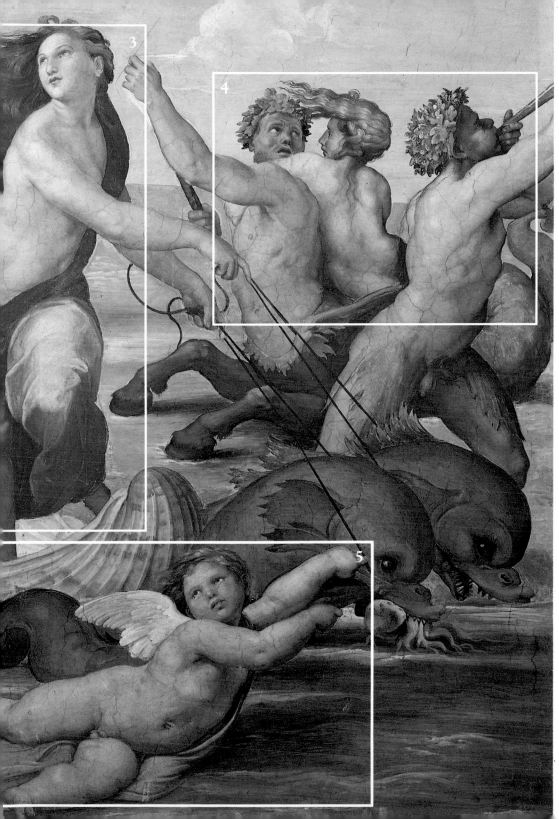

Raphael packed his composition with lively motion.

1. On the far left, a triton bends his head backward while blowing on a shell. The horse twists its head in the same direction.

2. This triton, embracing a nereid, is a fantastic combination of parts. He has the trunk of a man, the pointed ears of a donkey, and the tail of a fish!

3. Galatea commands the center of the composition. Her partially draped figure and her balanced pose make her resemble a classical statue of Venus.

4. This horn-blowing triton stretches out of the picture, while the one behind him reaches toward the middle of the composition. Raphael loved to show bodies twisting in opposite directions.

5. Little Palaemon's graceful body echoes Galatea's as it sweeps across the bottom of the painting.

The Deliverance of Saint Peter from Prison

Pope Julius II wanted a series of grand rooms in his private quarters in the Vatican, where popes traditionally lived, to be redone in the latest style of the Renaissance, and he hired many artists to work on them. Among the artists who were asked to paint murals and decorations was Raphael. Within a short time, he was put in charge of all the rooms. These chambers were very large, with great circular arches and vaulted ceilings. It took him a little over two years to complete the first one.

In the Vatican murals, Raphael portrayed scenes from history and important moments in the lives of former popes. One painting had as its subject the first pope, Saint Peter. It showed his miraculous escape from prison, a story that had special meaning for Pope Julius II. Before he became pope, his own church in Rome was where the prison chains that had bound Saint Peter were preserved and venerated by the pious. During Julius II's papacy, invading French troops threatened Rome. The pope made special visits to the precious relics of his old church, and the troops were eventually driven from Italy. The pope felt that both he and the church had been delivered to safety, just as Saint Peter had been.

The wall on which Raphael painted the story about Saint Peter contained an alcove. The wall was also half round, with a thick stone arch around it. Because the architecture could not be changed, the artist used it as part of his design. Raphael constructed a semicircular picture to work around the awkward shape, integrating the actual structure of the room into the painting to make the scene look realistic. The stairs he painted on either side of the alcove are so convincing that they seem to penetrate the wall. Above the alcove, Raphael created a prison cell with iron bars across one side. Another of the artist's startling effects is the way he made the soldiers on the left side of the painting look as if they are coming out from behind the arched stone frame.

Light Conquers Darkness

Peter, a disciple of Jesus, led the first Christians. The New Testament reports that Herod, king of Palestine, often persecuted them, and eventually put Peter in jail. Peter was a prize captive, so four squads of soldiers guarded him. Although he was bound with two strong chains, a pair of sentries stayed in his cell to prevent him from escaping. While Peter was sleeping between these men, "an angel of the Lord appeared, and a light shone in the cell." The angel woke Peter, and the chains fell off his hands. Then Peter followed the angel out of prison, even though he thought he was seeing a vision. Three parts of the story are shown as though they are all

happening at once. Raphael took the opportunity to rely on contrasts to make his story dramatic. The deep blackness of the prison bars makes the brilliant light that radiates from behind the angel seem as bright as that of molten metal. The caution of Saint Peter and the angel as they quietly leave the prison contrasts with the careless sprawl of the guards across the stairs. Other contrasts are the calmness of the angel with the agitation of the captain of the guard, and the fear of his soldiers with the faith of Saint Peter.

LEFT:
Raphael suggested the dark of night by contrasting the black iron bars with the brilliance of the angel's radiant light. Similarly, the scene's dark shadows contrast with the reflections from the soldiers' armor. The large wall on which the artist painted this subject is above eye level, so he worked with perspective to make it seem as if the viewer were standing below, peering into a jail cell.

RIGHT:
The snoring soldiers, whose faces are hardly visible, will not be awakened by the gentle passage of the angel and Saint Peter.

FAR RIGHT:
The story's tranquility is broken when the soldiers discover that their prize prisoner has escaped. The posture of the soldier in the foreground suggests that he is barking a command loudly at his dazed subordinate.

A remarkable woman named Elena Duglioli was famous in Italy for her visions. She modeled her life after the early Christian saint Cecilia. Having been given a bone from Cecilia's body, Elena started a cult around this holy woman.

Elena had a vision in which she saw an altarpiece, and she commissioned Raphael to paint it. The altarpiece was meant for a chapel in Elena's local church, where the relic of the saint was kept. She asked that Saint Cecilia be in the center of the painting. Raphael complied. He put Saint John, Elena's special patron, behind Cecilia's right. Saint Paul, the energetic writer and missionary, stands at the far left, leaning on his sword. Saint Mary Magdalen, one of the Bible's most famous converts to Christianity, is opposite. Between her and Saint Cecilia is Saint Augustine, another convert and the patron of the priests of Elena's church.

Broken Instruments and Angel Voices

Traditionally, saints are recognized in paintings by the symbols, or attributes, they carry. Four such symbols are conspicuous in Raphael's painting. Saint Paul carries his glistening sword and pages from one of his sermons. Saint Augustine's staff, with a fantastic creature in its crook, is a miniature sculpture made of precious metals.

Evangelist, Augustine, and Mary Magdalen

Called a crosier, it is the sign of a bishop. Saint Mary Magdalen carries the jar of perfume with which she once bathed Jesus's feet. Its polished surface reflects her hand. She is the only saint who makes contact with the viewers as she turns her beautiful face toward us. The final attribute, Saint Cecilia's pipe organ, is the key to the uplifting lesson that the painting teaches.

Holding a portable organ in her hands, Saint Cecilia lets the pipes fall out. Soon they will be on the ground with an array of other musical instruments. The viola da gamba, the ancestor of the cello, has lost its strings and is badly battered, and so are some of the other instruments near it. But the saints do not mind. They are engrossed in other music, the sounds from the angelic chorus in heaven above. The altarpiece shows what Elena Duglioli believed—that a holy life opens up beauties more wonderful than even the most beautiful sounds on earth.

Because he had so much work to do, Raphael hired artists to assist him. One of them, Giovanni da Udine, painted the musical instruments at the feet of the five saints. How wonderfully realistic they are! The two female faces were done by Raphael himself. Saint Mary Magdalen is singled out for her beauty, and Saint Cecilia, for her expression of transport. One writer, thirty years after Raphael's death, said "Let others paint the face alone, reproducing it with colors. Of Cecilia, Raphael has shown the face and soul."

33

The Miraculous Draught of Fishes

From Cartoons to Silk, Silver, and Gold

By the time he was thirty-one years of age, Raphael was given charge of all the art created and preserved in the Vatican. By then he had a large workshop of apprentices to help him. The Sistine Chapel was now in his charge. It was the place where the pope worshiped in private and where he met with officials. Over the years, it had been decorated by the most famous artists in Italy. Now it was Raphael's turn to adorn the splendid room. For its walls, he designed a set of ten tapestries that were woven by the finest weavers in Europe in threads of silk, silver, and gold.

Raphael painted his designs on paper, making them exactly as big as the finished tapestries would be, about eleven feet high and thirteen to seventeen feet wide. Called cartoons, these paintings were what weavers looked at through the threads of their looms as they copied the designs. Because the weavers faced the back sides of their work when they wove, the finished tapestries were the mirror images of the cartoons. For instance, in the cartoon for *The Miraculous Draught of Fishes*, Jesus is blessing people with the wrong hand—the left hand—because Raphael knew that the weaver would reverse it. The tapestry shows Jesus lifting his right hand in the correct, traditional way. Raphael already knew how to compose backward because he had created designs for mosaic makers and engravers who also reversed their patterns.

Raphael's cartoons illustrate stories from the New Testament, and a number of them are about Saint Peter, from whom the popes inherited their authority. *The Miraculous Draught of Fishes* illustrates a story that took place when the future saint was a fisherman and had just finished a long but fruitless night at sea. Nonetheless, Jesus instructed Peter to "launch out into the deep, and let down your nets for a draught."

Peter explained that there were no fish, but obediently did as he was told. As soon as the nets were in the water, they filled up with so many

After Raphael
This is one of the tapestries woven from Raphael's cartoon.

35

fish that they broke. Other boats had to come to help. Astonished, Peter knelt before the miracle worker. "Depart from me," he begged, "for I am a sinful man." Jesus answered, "Fear not; from henceforth you shall catch men." Peter and his companions then abandoned their boats and followed Jesus.

Raphael pictured the moment in the story that marks the start of Saint Peter's life as a Christian minister, bishop, and pope. On the left, Jesus calmly blesses Peter, making him a catcher of men, that is, a missionary. To connect Saint Peter to Rome, the city of the popes, Raphael showed parts of it in the background. He included Saint Peter's church, which houses the bones of the fisherman saint. It is just over the shoulder of the man who holds out his arms in amazement at the power of Jesus. He is James, a partner of Peter. The rest of the boat is filled with fish.

The other half of the cartoon shows two fishermen trying to take up another draught of the sea creatures. The rippling muscles of their backs and arms indicate that their net is full, too. All the faces in the painting are turned toward Jesus, directing the viewer's eyes there as well. Raphael surrounded Jesus and Peter with more space than the other figures, so they become the center of attention even though they are on the left side of the cartoon.

37

Portrait of Baldassare Castiglione

The Courtier

Kings, dukes, and other rulers had retinues, or courts, to assist them. The members of a court were called courtiers, and among them were relatives of the ruler, others of noble birth, and high-ranking officials and servants. Baldassare Castiglione wrote a book about a courtier's etiquette and education. Called *The Courtier,* the book is a vivid account of Renaissance life and ideals. It was inspired by the court of Urbino, where Castiglione later served as a diplomat. The book became a standard manual of behavior in many of the courts of Europe.

Baldassare Castiglione was five years older than Raphael and throughout his life was one of his closest friends. He was best known for his diplomatic and political missions for the duke of Milan, the duke of Urbino, and the popes who reigned during his career. Castiglione's work frequently kept him far from his home in Mantua. These unhappy absences were probably what prompted him to ask Raphael to paint his portrait. He wanted the painting so that his wife and son would remember him while he was away.

A Pose That Speaks

Raphael made Castiglione's image life size. He chose an unusual pose, one invented by his older contemporary, Leonardo da Vinci, in a famous painting called the Mona Lisa. The usual way of showing a person was to turn the body and head toward the viewer. But Raphael turned Castiglione's body away from the viewer and rotated his head the other way, so that he looks straight out of the painting. Although this pose is like the Mona Lisa's, there is nothing in Leonardo's painting like Castiglione's exaggerated sleeve. It thrusts out, placing the courtier as close as possible to the frame of the picture.

In his book, Castiglione recommended sober colors for clothing. The pink of his skin and the blue of his eyes are the only relief from the subdued blend of black, white, gray, and brown in his portrait. Raphael also placed touches of gold in the pin in his cap and the button of his jacket, but he muted such details so they would not distract from the face. He enlivened the billowy gray sleeves and front of the jacket by recording every variation in the play of light on the fur's pile. Against these almost infinite shades, the black of the garment and cap are flat and unvaried. Their curving contours and jagged cutouts frame the intelligent face of the sitter. Castiglione's sloping arms and puffed-out chest form an ample triangular base for the oval shape of his bearded face and circular cap. The white shirt and black collar lock the upper and lower parts of the portrait together.

The Vision of Ezekiel

In the biblical days of Daniel, Jeremiah, and Nebuchadnezzar, a priest named Ezekiel was called by God "to be a watchman unto the house of Israel . . . to give them warning" from God (Ezek. 3:17). To usher Ezekiel into his life as a prophet, God appeared to him in a whirlwind of fire preceded by four creatures, each with four wings and four faces. The faces were those of a man, a lion, an ox, and an eagle. These faces also represented the writers of the first four books of the New Testament, which are called the Gospels. Raphael simply showed God being swept toward earth amid the winged symbols of the four sacred writers: a man for Saint Matthew, a lion for Saint Mark, an ox for Saint Luke, and an eagle for Saint John. The artist also included two pudgy putti under God's arms.

Raphael did not neglect the descriptive words of the Bible. The backdrop for Ezekiel's vision was burning fire the color of amber. Raphael portrayed it as a brilliant light. The Bible says that Ezekiel fell to his face when he saw the vision, but God commanded him to rise and gave him his assignment to be a prophet. This is the moment that Raphael pictured. With arms outstretched, God looks down at a tiny figure. Rays from clouds in the lower left corner of the painting illuminate Ezekiel. God the Father's left arm and the slope of his lap form a diagonal that leads to the diminutive figure of the great man. The painting itself is on a wood panel under twelve inches wide.

The Divine Mark of Geometry

Although God's outstretched arms bless Ezekiel, they also seem to slow the speed of his descent. His flying hair, the billowing of the rose drapery that covers him, and the flapping of the angel's robe are other signs of motion.

In art, the symbols of the Gospel writers were almost always placed in a frame around Jesus, Mary, or God the Father. Raphael ignored that tradition and made them form a throne supporting God the Father. The angel's wings perfectly balance the lion's wing below and the two wings that stretch out from the ox and eagle. An imaginary line linking the tips of the outermost wings, the foot that touches the lower cloud, and the fingers of God the Father would result in a perfect square.

Renaissance artists made stories from the Bible and ancient history come alive through their ability to paint realistic people and settings. They also used geometry to construct their compositions, knowing that the Greeks believed geometry was a key to the mysteries of the universe. Raphael's use of a square, one of the most perfect of geometric shapes because it is equal on all sides, gave a divine mark to his small painting.

The Transfiguration

The New Testament relates that Jesus once took three of his disciples, James, John, and Peter, to a high mountain. There, he was changed, or transfigured. His clothes glowed the whitest of whites and his face became radiant. Jesus was joined by Moses and Elijah, who had long been dead but

were now talking to him about his death. A voice came out of a bright cloud that surrounded them and said to the disciples, "This is my beloved Son, in whom I am well pleased; hear ye him." Stunned, the disciples fell down. To them, the dazzling appearance was a glimpse into the future revealing the glory of Jesus in heaven after his work on earth was done. As Jesus returned from the mountain, he encountered a crowd. Amid the gathering were his other disciples, who were trying without success to cure a boy filled with evil spirits. They turned to Jesus, who said, "All things are possible to him that believeth." With that, he sent the devil out of the child.

Raphael was commissioned to combine these two scenes in an altarpiece ordered by Cardinal Giulio de' Medici for the cathedral in Narbonne, France, where he was bishop. The cardinal was one of Raphael's most illustrious patrons. He was also a cousin of the new pope, Leo X, and the pope's closest adviser. Both men were members of the powerful Medici family of Florence. *Medici* is the Italian word for "doctors." Thus, an altarpiece that points to Jesus as the great doctor, or *medicus*, in Latin, flattered the family.

Although the New Testament accounts of the Transfiguration do not mention that anyone's feet left the ground, Raphael pictured the three

holy men rising up. Moses, holding the tablet with the Ten Commandments on it, faces Jesus from the left. Elijah grasps the book he wrote

foretelling the life and death of Jesus. The two kneeling figures on the far left are saints to whom the Cathedral of Narbonne is dedicated.

Raphael's Last Painting

Raphael pictured the possessed child supported by his parents. His eyes roll back in his head and his arms stretch wildly up and down. His mother and father implore the disciples to help him. The magnificent woman kneeling in the center of the painting challenges the followers of Jesus to heal the youth. The disciples look at the child with a variety of expressions. Some show compassion, others worry. They cannot understand why they have had no luck in delivering him from the evil spirits. Two of them, however, point to Jesus. They are joined by a member of the boy's family, who also lifts his hand toward the great physician.

The Bible separates the two episodes by a day, but Raphael made them occur at the same time. The uplifted hands link the two parts, and so do strong contrasts. All the figures in the lower half of the altarpiece emerge out of darkness. But above, the principal figures are bathed in light, with brilliant highlights making their costumes shine. The confusion surrounding the boy's plight makes the scene above seem all the more ordered and peaceful. This second contrast narrows the painting's focus to two figures, Jesus and the youth. The heavenly healer will lift the boy from a terrible life of darkness controlled by the devil, to a new one of faith, peace, and light.

Late in March 1520, Raphael became ill. For fifteen days, he suffered in bed. April 6 was his thirty-seventh birthday, and it was also Good Friday, the day that commemorates the death of Jesus. Raphael died that day. About thirty years later, Giorgio Vasari, an artist who wrote biographies of eminent artists, reported that Raphael was working on the face of Jesus in *The Transfiguration* altarpiece shortly before his death. The painting was placed at Raphael's feet as he lay in state in his studio. Cardinal Giulio de' Medici then decided to enshrine it above the high altar of one of the most important churches in Rome. His cathedral in Narbonne, France, only got a copy of it.

There was great mourning for Raphael. He was called "the prince of painters," and Vasari wrote that "when this noble artist died, painting died with him." In fact, Raphael's paintings inspired artists for centuries to come and were held as the highest standard of excellence. Every age borrowed from them and learned from them.

What Makes a Raphael

Raphael's compositions are harmonious. Here, groups of figures on one side of the painting balance groups on the other side. Raphael employed perspective to picture figures convincingly within a setting.

1. In creating the architectural setting, Raphael looked to ancient Roman models.

2. Sometimes the subject matter also came from antiquity. These two men are the Greek philosophers Plato and Aristotle.

3. The bodies are vigorous, muscular, and idealized.

4. Raphael's paintings are full of motion. Here, figures gesture, bend, step forward, and turn their heads.

2.

3.

4.